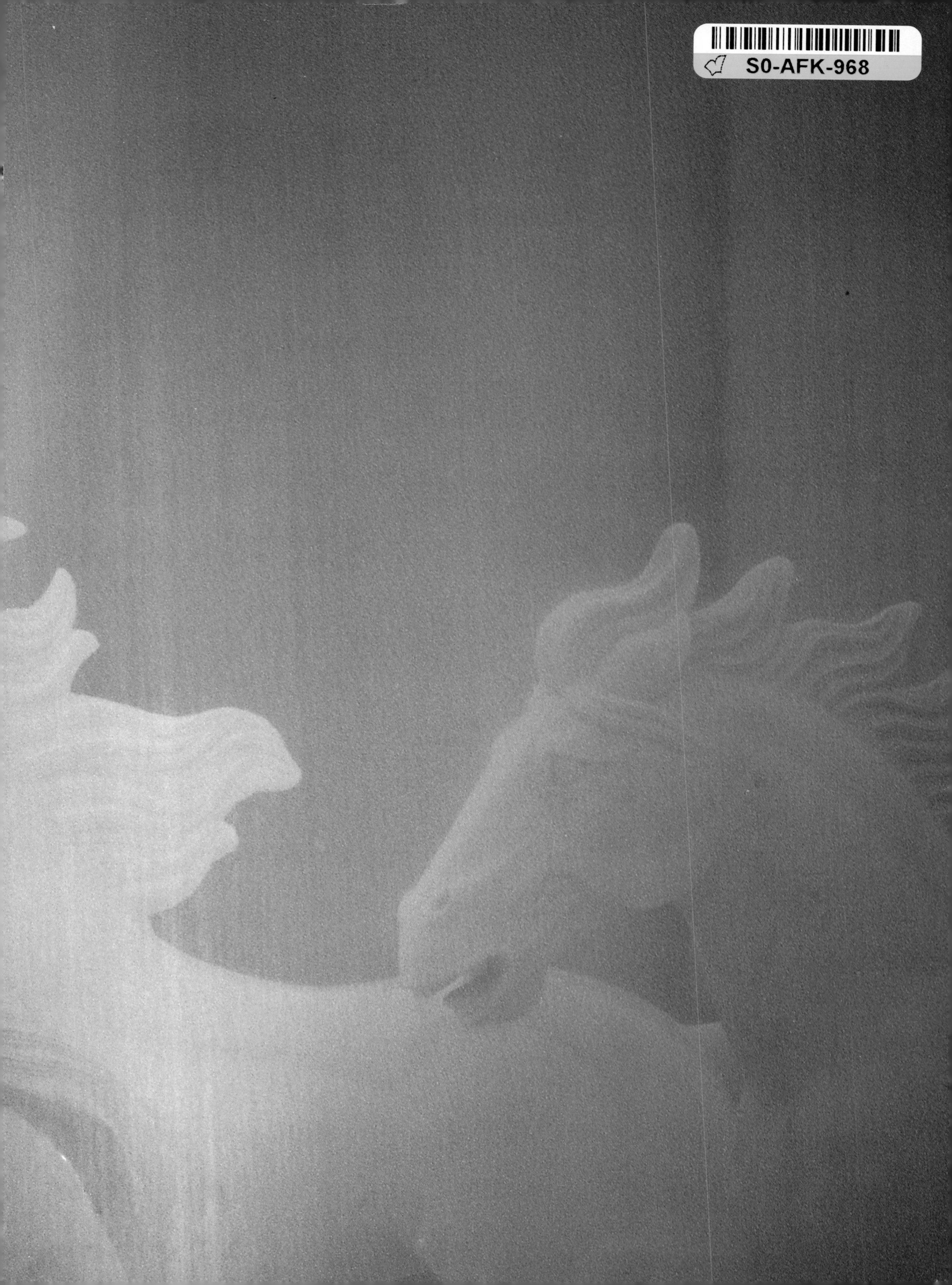

KAUAI
LAGOONS

Library of Congress Catalog Card Number 89-51853

ISBN 1-877690-01-5

First Printing, December, 1989

Series Editor: George Fuller

Series Design by Steve Shrader Graphic Design, Honolulu, Hawaii

The Westin Kauai Book Design by
Charles Taketa Graphic Design, Honolulu, Hawaii

Typesetting by Typehouse Hawaii

Printed through Times Editions Pte., Singapore

Printed in Singapore

KAUAI LAGOONS

Text by
JERRY HOPKINS & GEORGE FULLER

Photographed by
WILLIAM WATERFALL

Resort Publishers International
1990

CONTENTS

Christopher B. Hemmeter
Developer of The Westin Kauai

INTRODUCTION

Aloha!

It is with great pleasure that I welcome you to The Westin Kauai, one of the world's truly "Grand Resorts." I take special care, and pride, in the design and construction of a Hemmeter hotel. For me, a resort destination is successful only if it satisfies the most exacting criteria.

First and foremost, it must create a sense of experience. People want more than a room and a bed. Today's traveler is looking for revival, for newness, for the unexpected. The impact must be greater than the sum of the many parts.

It is my hope that we have created that forever memorable experience at The Westin Kauai. Eight miles of carriage paths and lagoons . . . an exotic wildlife program . . . two exciting shopping landings . . . the beachside ambience of Polynesia blending with the classic lines of European architecture . . . two Jack Nicklaus designed golf courses . . . a priceless art collection from Europe and Asia.

We have created a jewel, set in a mounting of exquisite beauty—with its gentle white sand beach, cool trade winds, and all the lush beauty that is Kauai.

However, a successful resort must also "recreate," for recreation is the truest of all experiences. It must allow its guests to revive emotions and feelings that have been dormant, to refresh the mind and soul, to give fresh life, to reanimate, to divert and amuse.

When a hotel allows its guests to create a new experience, while at the same time recreate old feelings of excitement, it is a winner.

This book includes an anecdotal history of the property on which The Westin Kauai sits—from the legends of the menehune, through the arrival of Captain Cook, followed a few years later by the missionaries, to today, and what you see as Hawaii's most unique destination resort.

This book also presents the hotel itself: the hotel as art and the hotel as art gallery. Through delightful photography and eloquent text we think that we have captured a truly "Grand Resort."

I'd like to extend my thanks and appreciation to all of the partners in this exciting project: VMS Corporation of Chicago, Kumagai Gumi of Tokyo, and Westin Corporation of Seattle.

Once again, let me welcome you to The Westin Kauai.

Enjoy!

Set against a backdrop of blue sky and surf, The Kauai Lagoons' wedding chapel is intimate and romantic. The wedding couple arrives in a specially decorated white carriage, pulled by matching dapple grey Percherons.

One of the most beautiful holes in golf, the 16th at Kiele is
formed atop a lava outcropping, bordered by the Pacific
Ocean and Nawiliwili Bay. Your score is (almost) less

KAUAI

The Garden Isle

THE GREENEST ISLAND

Kauai is by far the greenest of the Hawaiian Islands. Indeed, at Kauai's very heart is Mount Waialeale, whose summit is the wettest spot on planet Earth. Almost 500 inches of rain falls on the cloud-covered peak every year, and one look at the myriad waterfalls gushing down the sides of Waialeale, and it's clear why Kauai is called The Garden Isle—everything grows in its lush, marvelously tropical climate. The island even *smells* green.

There is an altar at the summit of Waialeale where the ancient Kauaian chiefs went, fighting their way through the wet, difficult terrain and blustery winds, to pay tribute to the most powerful of the old gods, Kane, the god of all living creatures. And it is from Waialeale that much of Kauai takes its shape.

Inland, on the west side of Mount Waialeale, is the untouched Alakai Swamp, a dense jungle where rare species of birds and plants flourish untouched. The north shore boasts the stunningly beautiful Na Pali coast, one of the world's incredible raw gems. The south side of the island is home to Waimea Canyon—which Mark Twain called "the Grand Canyon of the Pacific" when he visited in 1866—and the gentle beaches of Poipu. Kauai, in short, is an island of diverse and extreme beauty and quiet mystery.

This has not gone unnoticed by Hollywood. The jungles are used to shoot films about Vietnam, such as *Uncommon Valor*. This is also the island selected by movie makers for scenes of foreboding primitivism, as when King Kong came rampaging out of the greenery near Hanalei Bay . . . and heart-stopping romance, as when Rossano Brazzi sang to Mitzi Gaynor in a film called *South Pacific* on what today is called "Bali Ha'i" Beach.

Kauai is the fourth largest of the Hawaiian Islands, comprised of about 555 square miles of land. Yet fewer than 30,000 people live on the island, scattered in small villages along the irregular shoreline. It is estimated to be 5.6 million years old, the oldest of the chain. At one point, it is believed that Kauai and Niihau—the "forbidden island" which lies to Kauai's southwest—were one, and credence is given to that theory by the fact that the channel between the two islands is unusually shallow.

(Opposite page) On Kauai's north shore, the dramatically beautiful Na Pali coast features many inlets and caves accessible only by small boat. There is also a hike which takes the visitor through some of the most gorgeous scenery on the planet. (Photo by Franco Salmoiraghi)

Narrow ridges lead from Hanalei Valley to the foot of Mount Waialeale, which is capped by clouds for all but about six weeks of the year. The inordinate amount of rain at the summit—the plateau is the wettest spot on Earth—sweeps down the sides of the mountain, creating numerous waterfalls and the treacherous Alakai Swamp.

The Kalalau Valley, in the 1890s, was refuge to lepers who wished to escape deportation to the leper colony at Kalaupapa, on Molokai. Today, the valley is a popular destination for hikers along the Na Pali coast.

Dusk is one of the most beautiful times of day at Hanalei Pier, on Kauai's north shore. In the foreground is a 'hukilau' net, which has been used for gathering fish in Hawaii for centuries.

Emigration to Hawaii by a variety of peoples was the result
of a need for sugar plantation workers. In recent years, the
sugar industry in Hawaii has gradually declined.
Still, the importance of sugarcane cannot be downplayed.
Fields such as the one on these pages, with the Wailua
River running through it, are still in abundance throughout
the island chain.

Kauai's landscape is as spectacular as any in the world. On the south shore, near Poipu, is the famous Spouting Horn.

*Haena Point is the mouth of the Na Pali coast. The area has been
the setting for many Hollywood productions. Note the peak which
was used as Bali Ha'i in the film version of South Pacific.
It is a favorite fishing spot for locals.*

A golden sun silhouettes "the forbidden isle," Niihau, which lies off Kauai's southeast shore. In prehistoric times, the two islands were thought to be one. As evidence, scientists point out that the channel between the two land masses is unusually shallow.

(Opposite page) Hala tree, Princeville.

(Above) Spinner dolphins are resident off Kauai's coast. Visitors to
the island can swim with the dolphins in their natural habitat on
any number of organized sailing excursions. Most dolphins,
like the one pictured here, enjoy some playful showing off.
(Photo by James Watt)

(Following pages) Taro fields, like this one in Hanalei Valley,
have provided one of Polynesia's staples for centuries: poi.
(Photo by Scott Rutherford)

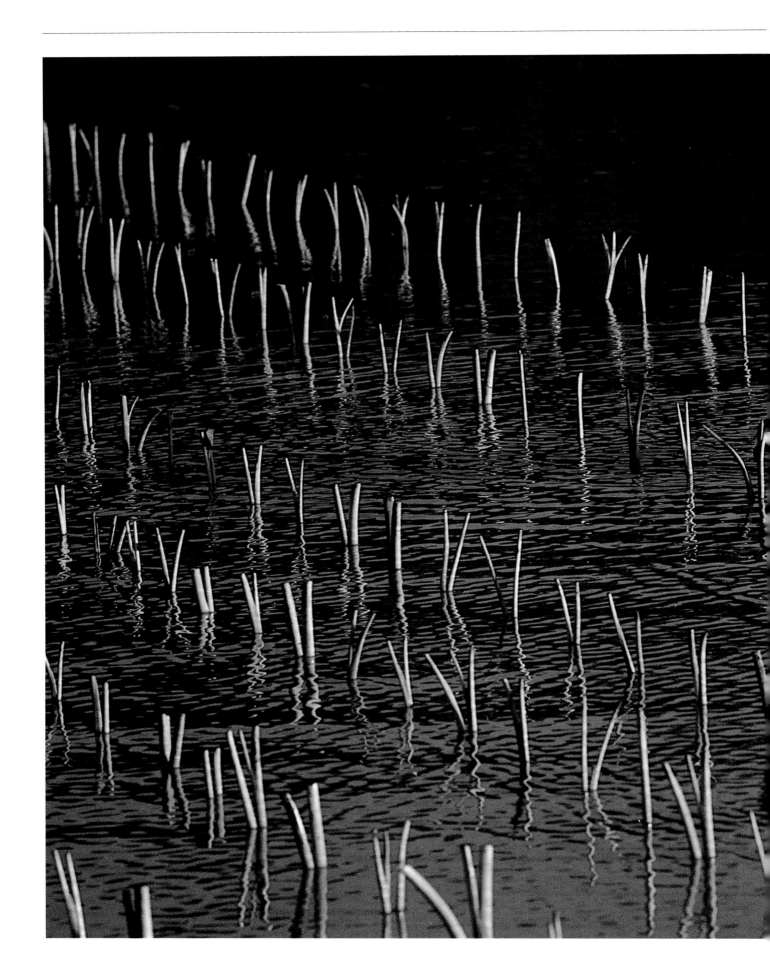

Fishermen are lured by the magic of a Kauai sunset.
It almost doesn't matter if you make the catch.

THE LEGEND
OF THE MENEHUNE

Kauai was where the menehune came, that mysterious race of "small people" who sailed north from Tahiti. Short and squat—and some legends say hairy—and very, very strong, they were said to work on projects only at night, using their great strength and vast numbers to accomplish mighty feats.

Sometimes they built hills solely for the purpose of rolling down them. They were musical, using bamboo nose flutes and Tahitian style hollow log drums. When they laughed, it was said that they made so much noise, they frightened the birds on Oahu.

In work, the menehune excelled as stoneworkers. They were said to have built the heiau near Wailua, as well as elaborate irrigation systems, such as the "Menehune Ditch," a job of fitted and dressed stonework that involved turning the course of the Waimea River and directing the water around a corner of a mountain. That accomplishment still draws respect from vacationing engineers.

They also built the Alakoko fishpond near Nawiliwili Bay, more commonly referred to as "Menehune Fishpond." The way the legend goes, a lazy man named Pi refused to help build a stone wall around the area which was to be used for the raising of taro and fish. Naturally, his chief refused to give him food in return for work not done.

That night, Pi wrapped portions of fish and poi and hung them in a kukui tree near the unfinished wall, knowing the menehune would find his offering when they came after dark to inspect the Hawaiians' work.

Pi was there to greet them, sweet-talking them into helping him finish the job. Soon, Pi was standing by as the little people passed stones from hand to hand, completing the wall before dawn. Next day, Pi took credit for completing the work and his chief sent him quantities of food and elaborate woven mats, proving that sometimes then, as now, there is no justice. Nonetheless, the fishpond remains, a few miles from Kauai Lagoons, giving the Nawiliwili Harbor area one of its most popular visitor attractions.

(Opposite page) Menehune were known for their proficiency on the bamboo nose flute, as were many early Hawaiians. (Limited edition serigraph, "Nose Flutes" by Elly Tepper, Banyan Editions.)

(Following pages) The Menehune Fishpond is one of the legends of Kauai. The menehune were rumored to come out only at night to build structures such as this one near Nawiliwili Bay.

*This drawing by Weber, on Captain James Cook's third voyage,
of an early Kauaian chief (hand-colored in modern day) is thought
to be Kaumualii, the last chief of Kauai.*

Cook's Arrival
and the Last Chief

It is generally agreed that the first inhabitants of the Hawaiian Islands sailed north from the Marquesas Islands, 2400 miles to the south, in double-hulled voyaging canoes. The exact dates of this initial migration are uncertain, but most archaeologists estimate that it occurred between 400-500 A.D., with a second migration around 1200 A.D. from Tahiti. Due to the ocean currents, the first land they reached is thought to be Kauai.

There is a good deal of evidence to support this Marquesan connection, including similarities in language, methods of farming and fishing, and the use of certain distinctive tools. One of these telltale implements was the stirrup-shaped poi pounder which was found only on Kauai and in the Marquesas.

It is possible that the Marquesans—and thus, by lineage, the Hawaiians—came through Asia, although the original Polynesian people bore no resemblence to the Asian people. Nevertheless, it is a pattern of migration which can be seen through the years, as the Hawaiian Islands became home to many diverse cultures. In the early years, travel between the islands of Polynesia, while by no means easy, was also not rare. Then, after 1200 A.D., for reasons lost to history, these voyages seemed to have ceased.

It must have been quite a surprise, then, in 1778, when a slight Englishman wearing white breeches and a blue coat with brass buttons sailed his huge ship, the *Resolution,* into Kauai waters. It was Captain James Cook, whose ships' sails were similar to the draped banners of tapa cloth that the Hawaiians hung from their own masts in honor of one of their primary gods, Lono. Thus, Cook was accepted by the Hawaiians as the reincarnation of their long-disappeared god Lono.

The natives who approached Cook's great sailing ships seemed almost shy. They were friendly, as evidenced by the fact that they carried no weapons, except for some stones, which they discarded after Cook convinced them that he meant no harm. The Hawaiians did not immediately come on board his vessel, but they did exchange gifts. Cook's men lowered some brass medals and pieces of iron on the end of a rope. The Hawaiians sent up fish and sweet potatoes.

Kauai was the first island of the Hawaiian chain which Cook "discovered" on his third voyage into the Pacific. His landfall was made at Waimea, about 30 miles from Kalapaki, and one can imagine how news of Lono's return must have traveled throughout Kauai and the other islands, conveyed from village to village.

Captain Cook, the British sailor who charted much of Polynesia
for Europe in the 1770s, was a humane explorer. It is through his
voyages—his journals, the journals of many of his voyage mates,
and the artists he took with him—that much of our knowledge of
early Polynesia is garnered.

Wherever he traveled on shore, the people, Cook wrote, "fell prostrate on the ground and remained in that position until we had passed." He attributed this reception as, "their mode of paying respect to their own great chiefs."

John Webber, the artist Cook had on board with him, recorded scenes of daily life in the village of Waimea, the sacred heiau, and several portraits of men and women. District chiefs, meanwhile, presented Cook with many gifts.

Within a year, though, Cook was dead, stabbed to death by natives at Kealakekua Bay on the Big Island after they stole a rudder from one of his ship's small launches, and he thought it "a good opportunity to show these people the use of firearms." They were "rather more surprised than frightened," he wrote in his journal. It was his final entry.

As the 18th century drew to a close, other white men from across the sea visited the islands, leaving venereal and other diseases behind them, wiping out huge chunks of the native population, whose immune system made it especially vulnerable.

At the same time, warring chiefs fought for control of the archipelago which Captain Cook had named the Sandwich Islands, often using the newfound weapons—guns—and foreign advisors. By 1796, Kamehameha the Great controlled the entire Hawaiian chain except for Kauai and Niihau.

Kamehameha claimed the failure of his first assault on Kauai was caused by a storm at sea which stopped his advance and killed many of his men. The warriors of Kauai said that that was nonsense, that a battle was fought and won—and they produced skulls from the sand to prove their point. Even today, bones are occasionally revealed by the wind and waves and shifting sands.

In 1804, Kamehameha planned a second attack, but this time his troops were decimated by an epidemic. So the attack was put aside for another six years when, in 1810, Kauai was finally won by negotiations and a little deceit.

Kaumualii, the king of Kauai, agreed to give his lands to Kamehameha so long as he, Kaumualii, remained the island's king. It was an empty title. In 1821, two years after Kamehameha's death, his son and heir Liholiho sailed to Kauai and invited Kaumualii aboard his vessel for dinner, suggesting he leave his warriors ashore. Kaumualii agreed and the ship sailed for Oahu during the meal. From that moment on, the king of Kauai was a prisoner.

Nine days later, Kaumualii was married to Kaahumanu, the favorite of Kamehameha's 21 wives, who had gained extensive power after Kamehameha's death. She then proceeded to also marry Kaumualii's eldest son, a Kauaian named Kealiiahonui who was reported to be almost seven feet tall. Through these manipulations, the Kamehameha dynasty gained title to Kauai. All the islands were now united.

(Following pages) Journal writing was quite an avocation with the early European explorers. These are two pages from Captain Cook's journals, written in December of 1778, wherein he describes his first contact with the people of Hawaii (which he refers to as "Owhyhee"; he refers to Tahiti as "Otaheite"). Cook seems clearly taken with the Hawaiian people whom he describes as "free from reserve and suspicion." Note the archaic use of an "F" in place of most "S"s.

As foon as day-light appeared, the natives afhore difplayed a white flag, which we conceived to be a fignal of peace and friendfhip. Some of them ventured out after us; but the wind frefhening, and it not being fafe to wait, they were foon left aftern.

In the afternoon, after making another attempt to weather the Eaftern extreme, which failed, I gave it up, and run down to the Difcovery. Indeed, it was of no confequence to get round the ifland; for we had feen its extent to the South Eaft, which was the thing I aimed at; and, according to the information which we had got from the natives, there is no other ifland to the windward of this. However, as we were fo near the South Eaft end of it, and as the leaft fhift of wind, in our favour, would ferve to carry us round, I did not wholly give up the idea of weathering it; and therefore continued to ply.

On the 20th, at noon, this South Eaft point bore South, three leagues diftant; the fnowy hills Weft North Weft; and we were about four miles from the neareft fhore. In the afternoon, fome of the natives came off in their canoes, bringing with them a few pigs and plantains. The latter were very acceptable, having had no vegetables for fome days; but the fupply we now received was fo inconfiderable, being barely fufficient for one day, that I ftood in

again the next morning, till within three or four miles of the land, where we were met by a number of canoes, laden with provifions. We brought to, and continued trading with the people in them, till four in the afternoon; when, having got a pretty good fupply, we made fail, and ftretched off to the Northward.

I had never met with a behaviour fo free from referve and fufpicion, in my intercourfe with any tribes of favages,

as

as we experienced in the people of this ifland. It was very common for them to fend up into the fhip the feveral articles they brought off for barter; afterward, they would come in themfelves, and make their bargains on the quarter-deck. The people of Otaheite, even after our repeated vifits, do not care to put fo much confidence in us. I infer from this, that thofe of Owhyhee muft be more faithful in their dealings with one another, than the inhabitants of Otaheite are. For, if little faith were obferved amongft themfelves, they would not be fo ready to truft ftrangers. It is alfo to be obferved, to their honour, that they had never once attempted to cheat us in exchanges, nor to commit a theft. They underftand trading as well as moft people; and feemed to comprehend clearly the reafon of our plying upon the coaft. For, though they brought off provifions in great plenty, particularly pigs, yet they kept up their price; and, rather than difpofe of them for lefs than they thought they were worth, would take them afhore again.

On the 22d, at eight in the morning, we tacked to the Southward with a frefh breeze at Eaft by North. At noon, the latitude was 20° 28′ 30″; and the fnowy peak bore South Weft half South. We had a good view of it the preceding day, and the quantity of fnow feemed to have increafed, and to extend lower down the hill. I ftood to the South Eaft till midnight, then tacked to the North till four in the morning, when we returned to the South Eaft tack; and, as the wind was at North Eaft by Eaft, we had hopes of weathering the ifland. We fhould have fucceeded, if the wind had not died away, and left us to the mercy of a great fwell, which carried us faft toward the land, which was not two leagues diftant. At length, we got our head off, and fome

3 Z 2   light

Another Weber print from Cook's voyages shows an early Kauai heiau.
These were sacred places where religious rituals took place.

*The Reverend and Mrs. William Harrison Rice, the first
permanent missionaries to Kauai.*

THE RICE FAMILY DYNASTY

Just as Kamehameha's rule was late to come to Kauai, so, too, were the missionaries from America. The first puritanical representatives of the Christian god, under the leadership of the Reverend Hiram Bingham, came to Hawaii to clothe and convert the heathen in 1820. They set up their mission in Honolulu.

In May of that year, two of the missionaries, Samuel Ruggles and Samuel Whitney, visited Kauai and established rapport with the Kauaian people. Both Ruggles and Whitney went on to spend part of their missionary careers in Kauai, as did others who followed them, but it wasn't until 1854 that the first permanent missionary family moved to Kauai—the Reverend and Mrs. William Harrison Rice.

There have been a handful of prominent and influential non-Hawaiian families who have set their imprint upon the island of Kauai over the years, and the Rice family must certainly be counted among them. A few were missionary families, and a few were businessmen's families. Some took their profits (or losses) and left. But some—the Rices, Wilcoxes, Fayes, Doles, Isenbergs, and a few others—found Kauai a loving home.

Of those families, it was the Rices who had the most to do with the development of Lihue, Nawiliwili Harbor and Kalapaki. Indeed, for many years, they owned most of the area. Like many of his peers, Rev. William Harrison Rice fancied the narrow whiskers identified with Abraham Lincoln and others of the time. They also shared many psychological traits, including a willingness to work hard, think good thoughts, and suffer in the cause of Christianity.

Six weeks before sailing from America, he had married Mary Sophia Hyde, the daughter of another missionary. They came with the ninth company of missionaries to Hawaii, arriving in 1840, and were assigned to a remote mission in Hana, Maui, where two daughters were born. The Rices served the Lord next on Oahu, where they taught for nine years at Punahou School, which had been founded to give the children of missionaries an eduction that was otherwise unavailable. There, another daughter and two sons were born.

In 1854, due to poor health and troubling finances, Rev. Rice retired from teaching and moved to Kauai to take a job as manager of Lihue Sugar Plantation. The job provided his family with a steady income, and, despite recurring illness,

*William Hyde Rice, the middle child of the five original
Kauai Rice offspring, was appointed Governor of Kauai by
Queen Liliuokalani in 1891.*

Rev. Rice continued to preach. His first congregation met in a grass house with a dirt floor. Eventually, his sermons were heard in a wooden church that he had had built, with seats and a bell.

The Reverend Rice died young, only 48 years old. Mary Sophia stayed on Kauai, where the Rice family could best benefit from the Reverend's hard work and foresight. Of his offspring, perhaps it was William Hyde Rice, the middle child of the five, who had the greatest impact on the island of Kauai.

At 25, he followed in his father's footsteps and married a missionary's daughter who was born in Tasmania, named Mary Waterhouse. William Hyde and Mary Waterhouse Rice lived on land that Rice purchased with his closest boyhood friend, George Wilcox, another missionary son. The land, consisting of thousands of acres located across the bay from where The Westin Kauai sits today, was purchased for $27,500 from Princess Ruth Keelikolani, one of the last descendants of Kamehameha I.

Like his father, William Hyde Rice spoke fluent Hawaiian and at an early age he started collecting native legends. In 1872, he formed Kipu Plantation and Lihue Ranch, and began concentrating on breeding cattle and fine horses. He is said to have cut a dashing figure with his full beard and long blond hair—looking very much like Buffalo Bill—as he rode across his open fields at a full gallop, reaching down from the saddle to pick up a coin on the ground as he passed.

Rice loved politics, serving 11 years in the State House of Representatives in the 1870s and 1880s—one of only three Caucasians to be elected to a predominately Hawaiian legislature. In 1891, he was appointed Governor of Kauai by his dear friend, Queen Liliuokalani, the last Hawaiian monarch. It was the Rice home, Hale Nani, at which the queen stayed during her first tour of the islands as monarch, also in 1891.

When the monarchy ended in 1893, with the house arrest of the queen, Rice adapted easily, serving his childhood friend Sanford Dole, who was named president of the new republic, and helped draw up the new constitution. The Rices, Doles and Wilcoxes were members of what one historian called the "haole (Caucasian) inner core"—the small group of missionary descendants, their relatives by marriage, and selected business associates who were determinedly grasping political control of the islands.

At the same time, they created a social environment that would grip local society in much the same way the Cabots and Lodges and others had dominated the social strata in Massachusetts.

The Rices had eight children in this world of pioneer privilege. The family home was a rambling, rococo-style structure in Lihue. But Rice also built a summer home on the beach at Kalapaki. By 1892, when the first photographs were taken, there were several small wooden structures connected by white board fences, giving the spread the look of a rural compound.

When William Hyde Rice retired to translate the Hawaiian legends he had collected throughout his life, management of the 6,000 acre Kipu Plantation fell to his son Charles, who developed the family's ranch into one of the territory's largest cattle businesses. At the same time, Charles acquired the Ford, Shell, and Goodyear franchises for the islands and thus was able to stay independent of the controlling sugar interests, even after being made manager of all the American Factor plantations on Kauai.

Charles expanded the summer home, named "Kalapaki" after the beach it sat on, to many times its original size. William Hyde Rice and Mother Rice had rooms in one end and there were additional bedrooms for the children and frequent visitors.

Kalapaki was known for its elegant hospitality, and visitors to the Rice home included many celebrities. The tobacco heiress Doris Duke, a part-time resident of Honolulu for many years, sailed into the harbor on her personal yacht. Opera great Lawrence Melchior was a houseguest, as was Louis Ferdinand, the grandson of the German kaiser, who was married to one of the Russian czar's nieces.

Charles Rice's wife died in 1940 and a year later he married Patricia Smith, a much younger woman who had served as a household nurse. In 1945, at age 69, Charles fathered his first son. Seven months later, on April 1st, 1946, one of the greatest tidal waves in Hawaii's history came roaring into Nawiliwili Bay and took everything away. The tsunami had already destroyed much of Hilo.

Charles was up early and had gone to work at the ranch when the giant wave hit. Patricia was at home with the baby. One of the servants, the gardener who doubled as chauffeur, was near the beach when he saw the water recede rapidly, a sure sign that a tidal wave was only minutes away.

He ran shouting to the house, then went to get the car. Patricia ran into the nursery and picked up the baby just as the wave hit the house, destroying it completely, taking everything uphill, depositing much of the furniture in the lily pond as it receded in a roaring wall back to the seething sea.

Patricia held onto the child as they were swept down the stream, approaching the small house of Keoma Ah You, which didn't even get wet. The two were pushed into a thicket of hau trees, where Patricia grabbed onto a large branch. A few minutes later, one of the Ah You children came out and pulled the mother and child to dry land.

The chauffeur was drowned and the car he was driving was lost. The furniture and fine wine, the china and silver, remained at the bottom of the lily pond or somewhere in the bay. Seven months later, an old feather cape net was found entangled among the roots of kiawe trees, but everything else was gone.

Charles Rice moved his family into a house on the ranch and Kalapaki was never rebuilt. Mrs. Ah You lived alone on Kalapaki Beach, a quiet neighbor to grazing horses and cows. And it would be many years before the area would play host to such an international set of personages again.

(Above) The Rice family on their porch at Hale Nani.

(Following pages) The site of The Westin Kauai was once the
Kalapaki Beach home of the Rice family. This photo was taken
around the turn of the century.

THE HOTELKEEPER

In 1953, Rita Hayworth and a crowd of Hollywood types visited the Rice property to film a few scenes for a movie based on Somerset Maugham's classic story about temptation, which he called "Rain."

Columbia Pictures took the name of the prostitute (played by Miss Hayworth) for the title of the film, *Miss Sadie Thompson.* The fire-and-brimstone minister who preached all the way up to his greatest sin was portrayed by Jose Ferrar.

There is disagreement about where the torrid scenes were filmed. Most say it was near the beach, not far from the home of Mrs. Ah You, who greeted the actors with flower leis and a cheery "Aloha!" whenever they came into view.

During the late 1940s and early 1950s, Kauai received few visitors. It was an unknown paradise, and even the increasing number of travelers who made their way to Waikiki rarely ventured as far afield as Kauai. But a paradise it was, especially on the northern and eastern shores, where the flora was thick and flowery. Hawaii's longest navigable river was on Kauai, Wailua, ending in a giant fern grotto. On the other side of the island was Waimea Canyon, a gorge not nearly as big as Arizona's Grand Canyon, but quite as spectacular.

These scenic secrets were known only to a few outsiders. Kauai was off the beaten track. And the people who lived on Kauai liked it that way.

In the 1950s, preservation of Kauai's rural lifestyle was not yet a political issue, as one day it would be, and from the time of the great tidal wave in 1946, up to statehood in 1959, Kauai was a tropical backwater so remote and determinedly anti-growth that it seemed of all the islands, it was the least ripe for commercial development.

And if it ever *did* develop, many thought the tourist industry would most likely develop on the north shore, near Bali Ha'i beach, where *South Pacific* was filmed. Others picked the region at the mouth of the Wailua River, where the Coco Palms hotel was opened in 1953, and where Elvis Presley filmed *Paradise Hawaiian Style* and *Blue Hawaii* in the 1960s.

(Opposite page) For the filming of The Hawaiians, *an elaborate set was constructed just south of Lihue, that was supposed to be Honolulu's Chinatown in the late 1800s. The set was used for many scenes in the movie, including the climatic Chinatown fire sequence. The star of the film, Charlton Heston, is seen in the center of the photo with the banded white hat. (Photo from* The Garden Island *newspaper)*

The old Kauai Surf Hotel, circa 1960.

Very few thought Nawiliwili Bay would become home to a world-class resort. Nawiliwili had, by the 1960s, developed into a bustling harbor, and the island's principal port. Between 1930 and 1940, it was used primarily by inter-island vessels, molasses tankers, lumber carriers and a few freighters taking out cargoes of canned pineapple. No one is quite sure why, but this facility was shelled by a Japanese submarine a few days after the attack on Pearl Harbor. After the war, the Lihue Plantation Company began shipping bulk sugar from an expanded dock and warehouse operation there.

Dudley Child, the president of InterIsland Resorts, was looking for a new location for his 64-room Kauai Inn, a cluster of two-story structures, then on the edge of Lihue. He knew, in the 1950s, as Hawaii inched toward statehood, that even on Kauai tourism eventually was going to provide great opportunity to hotelkeepers and anyone who wasn't on the beach was going to get lost in the rush.

One day, the assistant manager of the Kauai Inn, Bob Herkes, took his family to Kalapaki Beach to swim. Oddly, it was the first time anyone at InterIsland had ever been on the Rice family property.

The hills were covered with grass, weeds, and kiawe trees. Cows grazed in a swampy area, near where the Westin's Tempura Gardens restaurant is today. Two streams ran through the property and along the shoreline were thickets of hau and mango trees.

After walking the property, Herkes excitedly called his boss and said, "I found it! I found the place for the new hotel!"

Charlie Rice was 84 and he did not resist the chance to sell the land. A nephew, George Kimball, whose family had owned the Halekulani Hotel in Waikiki since the turn of the century, also made an offer. But InterIsland won the prize: 213 acres of history that stretched from the menehunes to Sadie Thompson, for only $613,000.

Child was counseled to keep his planned resort under two stories in height, but seeing the need for something larger, and grander, he built what became the island's tallest structure, the Kauai Surf. It poked 10 stories into the tropical sky, and contained a whopping 200 rooms.

Kauai had never seen anything like it. It was the first highrise outside Honolulu. It had Kauai's first passenger elevator. It was the island's largest electricity customer. And it was Kauai's largest employer.

By 1962, Child decided to increase the capacity of the Kauai Surf and get rid of the Kauai Inn. So he moved the five buildings of the Kauai Inn (each containing 12 to 16 rooms) by flatbed truck to the site.

Two years after that, he constructed another 100 rooms next to the existing highrise, and simultaneously sold the cottages. Child tried to buy Mrs. Ah You's home on the beach, but ownership of the small frame cottage and land, a gift of the Rice family, was never transferred. Mrs. Ah You continued to sit on her lanai, making leis, happily greeting the hotel guests, becoming an asset after all.

The number of visitors to Kauai grew slowly. They were encouraged to tour the island's scenic wonders, following the same route in Child's rented cars that William Hyde Rice had once taken by horseback with Hawaii's last queen, Liliuokalani. The hotel had a 42-foot catamaran for sunset cocktail cruises and in 1970, added several rowboats, pedal boats and other small craft to the inventory, so hotel guests could explore the Niumalu River on the other side of Nawiliwili Bay. Still, there wasn't much to do. The residents liked it that way.

THE HOTEL IS AN ART PIECE

*The Westin Kauai's remarkable Palace Court Reflecting
Pool: Fantasy and luxury set within a natural paradise.*

BUILDING MONUMENTS TO MANKIND

Hawaii was a new state when Christopher Bagwell Hemmeter stepped off the plane in 1960. He was from California, the son of an inventor. Like his father, he was a dreamer. Later, when some of his bigger dreams came true, the description would be upgraded to "visionary." He worked in Hawaii as a hotel management trainee during the summer of 1960, returning to permanently reside in the islands in 1962.

As a young man, Chris Hemmeter's dreams were mixed with ambition, and a desire to excel. When he was 10 years old he was earning as much as $400 a week selling Christmas cards door-to-door — in April! In school, he was elected class president from the sixth grade through the twelfth and was student body president of his grammar school and high school. His athletic accomplishments were numerous, including letters in a variety of high school sports.

After earning a degree at Cornell University's School of Hotel Administration, Hemmeter took his dreams to Hawaii, which had been a state for just a year. It was, for the thousands who came flowing in, a golden land of opportunity — and for someone in that most idyllic of verbal contradictions, the "leisure industry," the sunniest new frontier.

In 1964, with the help of his parents, Hemmeter borrowed $10,000 from the Bank of Hawaii to become a partner in a company established to develop restaurants in the Ilikai Hotel, then under construction. Two years later, he sold his interest in the business for a $14,000 profit and started another restaurant company, which he sold in 1968 for $1,500,000 in stock to a company which subsequently collapsed, rendering the stock worthless.

In the early 1970s, Hemmeter shifted his focus from restaurants to retail stores, naming his company and the stores for his two young sons, Mark Christopher, Ltd. Eventually there were 34 stores in the chain.

In 1972, he completed development of the King's Village in Waikiki, a multi-leveled shopping complex built in the Hawaiian monarchy style, taking much of its architectural inspiration from Iolani Palace, where Hawaii's last king and queen once reigned.

(Opposite page) Guests at The Westin Kauai can enjoy the hotel's huge swimming pool. On the other hand, beautiful Kalapaki Beach is just a few steps away.

All the while, Hemmeter clung to the dream of having his own hotel. As a teenager, he had visited the grand hotels in San Francisco and he never forgot the excitement he felt in the large, marble lobbies. Waikiki already had some great hotels—now it was time for a grand hotel. So he built a model of his idea, which he carried around to hotel chains to solicit their interest in operating his proposed hotel.

A young company named Hyatt was interested in managing Hemmeter's dream. So, to make room for what became the 1,234-room Hyatt Regency Waikiki, the chain's first-ever resort hotel—adjacent to King's Village—Hemmeter dynamited the 10-story Biltmore Hotel that stood on the site, after buying that property for $3,600,000. The hotel he then built, at a cost of $75,000,000, was the largest single private construction project in Hawaii's history and was the recipient of the world's second largest mortgage loan placed up to that time on a hotel development.

It was also the first Hawaii hotel to incorporate massive water features and one of the first to display art in a significant fashion. The huge open space between the two hotel towers was marked by a three-story waterfall and hanging overhead, and at the third-floor level, was an enormous metal sculpture.

Smaller sculptures, along with vases, paintings, priceless chests and other furniture, mostly from Asia, were placed carefully throughout the rest of the hotel—in the lobby, in hallways, in restaurants and cocktail lounges, in gardens, in the rooms.

"Originally," Hemmeter says, "I came up with the idea of art in hotels because I wanted to introduce a cultural element, to make a living museum, as opposed to just another structure. That intrigued me."

Two years after opening the Hyatt Regency Waikiki, Hemmeter topped himself with the Hyatt Regency Maui, then the most extravagant new hotel on the fashionable Kaanapali strip. Although the $68,000,000 cost was less than that of the Waikiki hotel, the complex system of streams, pools and water slides made this seem a far grander resort. It was the birthplace of the "destination resort" hotel.

Now there was art nearly everywhere the visitor looked. Flanking the entrance to the lobby were giant Chinese funeral urns. Filling a wing of the building were weapons, masks and statues from Papua New Guinea. Marking the convention center was a large, golden Buddha from Thailand. Parrots, penguins and royal carp enjoyed the giant atrium that took its name from a 30-foot banyan tree.

Hemmeter came to know many of the guests who stayed in his hotels, including two former presidents, Jimmy Carter and Gerald Ford. Carter and his wife Rosalynn became friends of Hemmeter and his wife, Patsy, and they frequently visited and traveled together. But it wasn't friendship that caused Carter to pick Hemmeter over a respected field of internationally renowned architects to design and build the Carter Presidential Library, Museum and Carter Center at Emory University in Atlanta. Again, it was the dream, the vision.

"The others mis-read President Carter," Hemmeter says. "They didn't understand him. They thought he wanted a monument to himself, but what he wanted was to give something back to mankind."

In 1984, Hemmeter sold his two Hyatt resort hotels to VMS, a Chicago real estate syndicate, for $316,000,000. Even before the sales had closed, Hemmeter heard that Dudley Child was selling his Surf hotels. He had wanted to buy the

Maui Surf and Kauai Surf hotels for some time, but all offers he made were turned away. Now, Hemmeter offered Child $94,000,000 for the two properties and brought VMS in as a partner.

"It was the location, that's all it was," Hemmeter says when asked why he chose to remodel two existing hotels after building two new ones. "People in the business were skeptical when they heard I had purchased the two hotels for $94,000,000 and was going to spend $350,000,000 remodeling them. But I knew there weren't going to be any more locations like these. Waterfront is very rare in Hawaii and prime waterfront is practically nonexistent.

"We're creating monuments to mankind, to the joy of life, to the majesty of the senses. We want our visitors to hear the music, not just the lyrics. Our destination resorts are created to heighten one's fantasies, to bring back the romance of life. We attempt to restore the grandeur that King Louis XIV must have experienced at Versailles.

"We attempt to understand people's dreams and expectations and develop experiences that turn them on. We attempt to exceed those expectations. We want our architects to be psychologists who understand the dreams and motives of our guests and who can respond accordingly.

"Our design sessions revolve around discussion of dreams and fantasies, of power and space, of romance and beauty, of plant life and animals, of art and culture, of quality and harmony and, oh by the way, of architecture!"

When night falls, the hotel's spectacular lighting makes a powerful aesthetic statement. The columns, trees and flowing water take on a whole new look.

It is magic that distinguishes a Hemmeter-developed hotel.
The floating vases at The Westin Kauai typify that magic.
Exhibited along the Colonnade above the swimming pool are
various types of vases, fish bowls and ginger jars—positioned
to appear as if they are floating on the surface of the water.

FANTASY & LUXURY SET WITHIN A NATURAL PARADISE

The Project Description filed with various government agencies in the months after Chris Hemmeter purchased the Kauai Surf made it clear where he was going.

"The applicant is proposing to make major improvements to the existing hotel as well as to construct additional facilities and amenities on the subject properties," Hemmeter said in his Kauai Surf Improvement Plan, submitted in 1985.

When word got out about what Hemmeter had planned for the old Surf Hotel, emotions were somewhat mixed. With sugar in decline on Kauai, as on the other islands, and tourism struggling to build momentum to replace it as a cash industry, there were many who defended his dream.

But there also were many who were dubious, clinging to the island's traditional no-growth or slow-growth philosophy.

In the end, it was Hemmeter's ability to convince the Kauai community that he believed in a quality hotel, which would stimulate the local economy and create new jobs, which pushed the project through. He offered one of the local canoe paddling clubs space to store canoes. And he enchanted the entire community with his fantasy.

"Hawaii doesn't need to build more hotel rooms," he said. "Hawaii needs to build more experiences."

Once again, water would play a major role. The Westin Kauai at Kauai Lagoons—as the 800-acre project came to be called—is home to Hawaii's largest swimming pool. One side of the pool is surrounded by five Jacuzzies, with nearby waterfalls flowing romantically 24 hours a day.

"I love to have landscaping that moves," Hemmeter says. "Water is like a mirror, constantly changing according to available light and the moving objects the mirror reflects. The sound of water is important, too. It blocks nearby conversations and provides a sense of privacy."

Waterfalls, too, are an important part of The Westin Kauai's landscape. "Waterfalls are intriguing because of their sound," Hemmeter says. "But there's more to it than that. There's a basic power and strength, very much like the waves of the ocean. I think that thrills most of us.

"It all relates to size," he continues. "Many people have swimming pools in their backyards. But we don't want to give them a pool like they have at home. We want to take it way beyond that. Size becomes a part of the definition of grandness.

"The human race has always put a premium on scale. The Pyramids are just thrilling structures! Washington, D.C., is monumental. The great capitals of the world are all the same. There is a grandness, a scale, a noble feeling."

Likewise, a Hemmeter resort puts a premium on grandness and scale. "Our primary goal is to give our hotel guests a sense of adventure and romance," he says. "We want to create the most special moments in their lives, the times they will look back upon and cherish."

Construction took more than a year and when the hotel opened, just 30 days after The Westin Maui, the old Kauai Surf was gone. The hotel with the small fleet of catamarans was replaced by Hawaii's first mega-resort.

There is a line in the song "Blue Hawaii" which says, "Dreams come true, in blue Hawaii . . ." Chris Hemmeter believes in fantasies, and for Hemmeter, that line would read, "Fantasies come true, in blue Hawaii."

(Opposite page) The magic of The Kauai Lagoons wedding chapel is highlighted by a gorgeous bed of purple bougainvillea.

The Kauai Lagoons Spa, located in the Golf & Racquet Club, offers guests European-style luxury services. These include Turkish steam rooms, saunas, weight training, massage, and the beautiful swimming pool shown above.

There is art everywhere. Here, guests play in the main pool,
while a pink marble turtle-dragon makes a nice fountain.

*The waterways of The Kauai Lagoons are traversed in specially
made Italian mahogany launches...*

...or privately, on captained gondolas. Either way, the leisurely
route through the lagoons is a special joy.

THE HOME OF THE GOLDEN BEAR

To a golfer, there exist in the world a few stunningly dramatic holes where the score is (almost) less important than the vista. The two Jack Nicklaus designed courses at Kauai Lagoons embody quite a few such memorable holes.

The Kauai Lagoons courses have been referred to as "the best golfing in Hawaii" by many aficionados of the sport. The Golden Bear himself has said of Kauai Lagoons' Kiele course, "This golf course is better from tee to green than Augusta National."

The course Nicklaus refers to—the Kiele—is a 7,100 yard, par-72 masterpiece which was designed to challenge even the pros. It is recommended for golfers with a handicap of 20 or better. Still, "better from tee to green than Augusta National" is quite a handle. And yet, when you play the course, you know exactly what he means. "On a scale of one to 10," Nicklaus said, "I'd rate the Kiele course a 13."

Not only is the course a golfers' challenge—such as hole 16, where the small green rests devilishly at the bottom of a hill backed by a treacherous drop-off into the ocean if you overshoot it—but at certain times of day, the light on Kiele is exquisite. Play it at first or last tee, and the picture becomes even clearer. Both the 15th and 16th holes rival Pebble Beach for sheer beauty, as they invite your eye to wander from the task of good golf to the rolling surf and marvelous views of Nawiliwili Harbor.

Kim Worrel, director of golf at Kauai Lagoons, said of Kiele, "This course was envisioned by Jack as Hawaii's greatest tournament course. Based on the overwhelming praise and delight of our golfers, I'd say he succeeded 110%. The Kiele is a challenging course, requiring length accuracy and a fine sense of touch on the putting greens."

Kiele translates loosely as "the sweet fragrance of the gardenia." With its spectacular scenery and design excellence, the course is, indeed, a sweet-smelling flower.

The second course—the Lagoons—was designed for players of all levels. Although it does not have the dramatic ocean front views, it is a beauty in its own right. At first tee, the early morning mists will give way to a few rays of sunlight and you'll find yourself in the midst of golf heaven. You're teeing off in isolation, watched only by a laughing Buddha, or a Chinese white marble tortoise.

(Opposite page) Sometimes even the Golden Bear himself—Jack Nicklaus—gets caught in a hazard. But then, he should know the way out of these sand traps—he designed them.

You see, the courses which Nicklaus considers art, also contain pieces of art as tee markers. Set upon 6,000-pound granite bases, these large marble tee markers are a unique concept, and one which is not found anywhere else in the world. There is the tortoise, Buddha, a rabbit, an eagle. Of course, there's also a golden bear. In fact, there is a different animal to welcome you to each hole.

The Lagoons is a Scottish links style course, which rambles over 6,900 yards of gently rolling fairways and well-contoured greens. "Our goal was to create a course where the players would have plenty of room to hit the ball," Nicklaus said of the Lagoons course, "and still find some exciting and fun-filled golf."

It is a goal which Nicklaus has clearly achieved. And, combined with the championship Kiele course, it is safe to say that Kauai Lagoons offers golf aficionados one of the best choices in the state of Hawaii.

*With two championship courses, both designed by
Jack Nicklaus, Kauai Lagoons offers some of the finest
golfing in the world.*

Horsin' Around

Next to Fergie, a 2500-pound dapple-gray Percheron, standing more than 19 hands tall, a person feels tiny. One of the largest horses in the world, Fergie is part of The Westin Kauai's collection of purebred draft horses—Percherons, Belgians and the more common Clydesdales, which most people know from beer advertisements.

With a total of 50 such brutes, the majority of which are Belgians, The Westin Kauai claims one of the largest working draft horse collections in the world. When you see them pulling the specially-made Landau carriages around the sprawling, 800-acre Kauai Lagoons property, you know you're in the presence of something unique.

Draft horses were originally bred for hard work—they *were* the machinery for early farming in Europe. Also, they were used for carrying knights in battle. Imagine how much a man in a full suit of armor weighs, and it's easy to understand the horses' size. In many cases, the horses were suited up in armor, too!

The distinctive embodiment of strength and spirit, horses are the true trademark of The Westin Kauai. From the untamed marble herd thundering through the fountain as you enter the Palace Court, to the oversized bronze replicas of Frederick Remmington sculptures at the Kauai Lagoons Fashion Landing, to the magnificent real beasts which trod the property pulling carriages, horses add a uniquely *paniolo* flavor to Kauai Lagoons.

Hawaiian cowboys—paniolos—are nothing new. The tradition of the paniolo in Hawaii dates back to 1803, when Captain Richard J. Cleveland brought several horses over from California as a gift for Kamehameha I. He deposited a mare and her foal on the Big Island—swimming them ashore—and, upon learning that Kamehameha had moved to Lahaina, sailed to Maui to present the remaining horses to the King.

Although it is reported that Kamehameha was none too impressed with the offering, for reasons lost to history, the introduction of horses to Hawaii—and of cattle a few years previous—brought a brand new lifestyle to the islands. Still today, the largest privately-owned ranch in the world is on the Big Island of Hawaii, the 225,000-acre Parker Ranch, now owned by the Smart family, which claims Hawaiian roots stretching back to Kamehameha I.

(Opposite page) Fergie, all 2500 pounds of him, is larger than life.

Sporting more than 50,000 head of cattle and 400 horses, Parker Ranch typifies a part of Hawaii which is not generally seen by visitors who stay near the sun-soaked beaches and swaying palms of the islands' coastlines: It is in the rolling green upcountry where you'll find Hawaii's cowboys.

Most of the early horses brought to Hawaii were Mustangs from the ranges of northern California, shipped over from the port city of Monterey. In an interesting twist of destiny, the horses brought in for The Westin Kauai, almost 200 years later, also were shipped from Monterey, albeit for much different reasons. Gathered in an equine sleuthing expedition which stretched across the United States, the horses which comprised the original Westin Kauai contingent were corralled in Carmel Valley (which is at the heart of Monterey County) at Stonepine Estate Resort equestrian center. They were then loaded onto Boeing 707s, two dozen of the huge beasts to a plane, accompanied by a veterinarian and handler, and flown to Kauai.

The trainers who traversed the country in search of the horses were Tommy and Debby Harris, directors of the equestrian program at Stonepine, and Denzel Cameron. Cameron, under Tommy Harris' direction, then moved to Kauai to train the drivers and handlers at the Westin. With a Hollywood background dating back to 1969, when he trained horses for the Clint Eastwood and Lee Marvin film *Paint Your Wagon*, Cameron went on to train horses for many other films. Some of the films he also acted in—sometimes a cowboy, sometimes an Indian, sometimes a soldier—but he is primarily known as a horse trainer *par excellence*. Perhaps his

The size of these draft horse's hooves is enormous.
In human equivalent: size 20.

best-known scene is the slow-motion sequence he coordinated in the film *The Man From Snowy River*, where horse and rider galloped down a foresty embankment so steep it appeared almost vertical, a scene of incredible power, skill and daring.

At The Westin Kauai, Cameron applied his horse sense to the training of grooms, drivers and stable hands. Although the tradition of the paniolo reaches into the roots of Hawaiian history, there were very few people in the islands who had experience with carriages, and almost none who had been around such *large* horses.

The Landau carriages are an interesting story. There are 37 of them, manufactured especially for The Westin Kauai in Bayfield, Ontario, Canada. They are exact replicas of the old Landaus which were used for transportation at the turn of the century, albeit with some modern safety features.

In fact, an antique Landau was dissected piece by piece, and then copied exactly to make the working model for the Kauai carriages. The builder, Tom Penhale, who has won many awards for his excellent work, had to greatly expand his facilities to handle the volume of the Kauai order. Surprisingly, though, there is still a great deal of carriage and wagon production being done in the United States and Canada, with most of the orders coming from the Amish in Ohio and Pennsylvania.

In addition to the 37 new carriages, The Westin Kauai also boasts five antique Landaus which are totally restored, and a six-up dray wagon which is used for special events and parades.

Special care was taken to ensure that these valuable animals adapted properly to the warm Hawaiian climate; pulling carriages all day is no easy task. Above, one thankful equine gets a welcome shower.

(Following pages) Thirty-seven specially made Landau carriages were created for Kauai Lagoons, offering guests the opportunity to take leisurely sightseeing tours of the 800-acre property.

An antique Landau carriage was dissected piece by piece to provide
the model for today's builders. In addition to the Landaus, there is
a six-up dray wagon which is outfitted for special occasions.

The horse handlers spend extra time and energy to ensure that each detail is just right, like this tail braid and flower ensemble.

THE
WILDLIFE PROGRAM

In a world where 75 acres of rain forest are being destroyed every minute, and where exotic birds and endangered wildlife draw rapidly nearer extinction, the preservation and propagation of threatened wildlife species has a new and innovative model. But if the combination of deluxe resort development and endangered species preservation seems an unlikely or incompatible proposition, it simply shows again that just about anything can happen at Kauai Lagoons.

There, the dreams of Christopher B. Hemmeter came together with the scientific careers of Wailua's Patrick and Mary Dunn to establish one of the most imaginative and unique wildlife programs in the hemisphere.

The introduction of exotic birds and fine art into the guest environment has become a hallmark signature in the design themes of Chris Hemmeter. Thus, it was the pursuit of enhanced guest experiences that led The Westin Kauai at Kauai Lagoons into the unlikely realm of zoology, aviculture, and the preservation and exhibition of endangered wildlife species.

Under the management of Patrick Dunn, with a staff of 10 keepers, the wildlife program at Kauai Lagoons is a world model for many zoos of the future. The lagoon, which itself is as distinctive as the wildlife program, consists of more than 40 acres of man-made waterways with six islands. On these islands, more than 200 rare and unusual species of birds and animals, including the Hawaiian state bird, the Nene Goose, live. There are also monkeys, kangaroos, wallabies, and many fascinating, often comical-looking birds.

Hemmeter, who with his son Mark, developed the plan and implementation of this totally unique visitor experience, previously worked with the Dunns on exotic bird programs at The Westin Maui, and the Big Island's Hyatt Regency Waikoloa. But the program at Kauai Lagoons is a zoological endeavor never before undertaken on such a grand scale by private enterprise.

(Opposite page) One of the lagoons' most popular residents is the African Crown Crane, whose distinctive hairstyle sets him apart from the crowd.

107

Unlike their Caribbean counterparts, the Chilean
Flamingoes can be found from sea level to several thousand
feet into the Andes Mountains. Their color is less pink than
their coral pink "Miami Vice" cousins whose native habitat,
which once ranged throughout nearly all of the Caribbean,
is now limited to the Yucatan Peninsula in Mexico and zoo
parks in the tropics.

This sextet of African White-Faced Tree Ducks is equally at home in the water or in the trees. It is one of the few duck species which nests in tree branches.

The black-faced Colubus Monkey makes its home on Monkey Island. It is the longest-haired monkey of the species. There are four of them at Kauai Lagoons.

THE HOTEL
IS AN ART GALLERY

THE WESTIN KAUAI COLLECTION

Hawaii is, by virtue of its geographic location, a link connecting the vast continent of Asia to the West. In this way, The Westin Kauai at Kauai Lagoons showcases the unique quality of the Hawaiian Islands through the blending of Western design with Asian and Pacific art forms.

Among the cultures represented in The Westin Kauai Collection are those of China, Burma, Thailand, India, Japan, and Kampuchea (Cambodia). The collection also includes more familiar forms of art from Europe, Hawaii, and the Mainland United States.

There are more than 3000 individual pieces of art on display, making The Westin Kauai Collection one of the largest privately held collections in the world. The collection ranges widely, in both form and style. As you enter the porte cochere, you are greeted by a large marble healing Buddha from China. As you descend the escalator into the Palace Court, Burmese winged lions and gold lacquered Thai fish vie for your eye's attention with a herd of white marble horses charging through the fountain, a sculpture inspired by the Palace at Versailles.

Throughout, The Westin Kauai at Kauai Lagoons offers guests and visitors an experience unique in the world. The resort sits in one of the Hawaiian Islands' most beautiful settings. It also exhibits a sensational concept in resort design, a design which is enhanced by a diverse and truly fascinating collection of art.

Art in public places is not a new concept. Office buildings, public parks, school campuses, shopping centers—no matter where you go today, you will find art and sculpture displayed.

But The Westin Kauai is considerably more than that. It is, in itself, an art piece. As you walk through the resort, you will see elaborate water fountains, Grecian-styled columns, shimmering chandeliers, and architectural touches from many corners of the world.

The Westin Kauai is also an art gallery, and this *is* a new concept. The resort's designer/developer, Christopher B. Hemmeter, has made the display of art one of his remarkable signatures, believing that the presence of art will enhance each guest's stay. It is a philosophy which Westin Corporation is proud to share.

The scowling wooden sculpture above is actually
a guardian figure. Warriors such as he often escorted Buddha in life,
and today guard his temples.

(Opposite page) In the garden adjacent to Palace Court is a
stylized marble poi pounder by Hawaii artist Sean K. L. Browne.
It was inspired by much smaller, hand-held stone implements used
for pounding cooked taro root into an edible, paste-like poi.

The Chinese are known for their enamelled brass, or cloisonné. Two excellent examples of this colorful art form are the large vases at the base of the escalator as you first enter Palace Court. The flower detail on these pages is from one of those vases.

122

*This Japanese silk painting of three deer has all the characteristics
of the best Japanese art: excellent craftsmanship, quality materials,
and a sense of serenity.*

*Christopher R. Hemmeter (foreground) negotiating the prices
of art in northern China. On this particular night, the lights went
out in the entire district, necessitating candlelight bargaining.*

THE ART OF COLLECTING ART: FROM BANGKOK TO CANTON

Christopher B. Hemmeter is best known as the developer of fantasy resorts. His projects, such as the Westin Kauai, have earned him a reputation as a visionary. And yet what is it that makes The Westin Kauai so spectacular?

Imagery. A team of white marble horses thundering through a vast reflecting pool, their hooves pounding the water 70 feet into the air. A laughing Buddha welcoming you to the fourth hole on a rolling green golf course. Or a flock of pink flamingoes gracing an island in the middle of a gently winding lagoon. It is imagery which speaks to the romantic in each of us. Imagery which tells us that the resort itself is a piece of art.

Today, most of the collecting—and the commission of original art—is done by his son, Christopher R. Hemmeter. From a small factory surrounded by rice fields in Taiwan he commissions some of the largest ceramic vases ever produced— 10-foot replicas of 12-inch originals found in Chinese palaces during the Ming and Ch'ing Dynasties (1368-1644, 1644-1911 A.D.).

From the Sepik River basin in Papua New Guinea—the last place on earth to be "discovered" by the modern world—comes a collection of rare ritual masks.

Although much of the artwork in the collection is new—produced by commission specifically for The Westin Kauai—there are also many pieces which are quite old. Discovered in antique stores, or acquired from individuals who have had them in their families for generations, many of the older items are religious in nature, remnants from palaces and long-gone temples.

Because the first large-scale stone sculpture was produced in China during the Han Dynasty (202 B.C.-220 A.D.), the Hemmeters traveled to Yang Ping, the small village near the Mongolian border where green, black, rose and white marble has been carved for 2000 years.

There, the great marble blocks are still pulled by hand out of the quarry, then hauled by donkey to an open field where stone carvers have carefully turned stone into art for 80 generations. Frequently, Hemmeter and his associates must struggle to make themselves understood, as in these remote locales, English is almost never spoken. Sign language is common, the message is conveyed, price is negotiated (with even more robust sign language), and the fabulous pieces of art are created for your viewing pleasure at the magnificent Westin Kauai.

The Art of Collecting Art:
CHINA

(Opposite page) Chinese marble carver.

(Following pages) A typical early morning street scene in Tan Jin.
Most everyone commutes via bicycle.

A Visit to the Marble Mines

For 2000 years, from the time of the Han Dynasty (206 B.C. to 220 A.D.), marble has been mined and carved in the tiny village of Yang Ping on the tough, high plains of Northern China near the Mongolian border.

Here, in Chiu Yang County, Hebei province, amazing marble tributes to Buddha and his disciples and Chinese figures of the zodiac are carved in huge yards operated by the Qu Yang Third Stone & Wood Sculptures & Carving Factory. This is a company that has 350 stone-carvers on the payroll, some of them descendants of stone-carvers from the days of the Han Dynasty.

Only a little has changed since then. The village is still comprised of small houses made of mud and stacked stone, and the streets are barely wide enough for a single vehicle. Crude ladders lead to the flat roofs where corn and other food is dried in the bright sunlight and crisp air. Water is pulled from a well and rice is milled on a large, flat marble plate with a heavy marble roller. There is no plumbing or electricity.

The quarry is located less than a mile away in what used to be a medium-sized mountain and now is only a large hill. It is called Yellow Mountain and it is here that the thick, solid veins of white, pink, green and black marble are mined. The work is difficult, primitive.

When the three- and four-ton blocks of stone are knocked loose and fall to the bottom of the quarry's 40-foot pit, it is manpower that hauls the marble out. A strong metal cable is carried into the pit and tied around the huge rock. It is taller than the men who are tying it up, about half the size of a large bus. The other end of the cable is tied around a short post at the top of the hill. There is a long cross-piece at the top of the post, a 20-foot pole, affixed to the post with a bolt. Fifteen men line up next to the pole, half on one side, half on the other, and they start pushing the pole, walking in a circle, wrapping the cable around the post, until the marble boulder is raised.

The big rock is then manhandled with more long poles serving as levers into a donkey cart, then it is taken two miles to the "factory," a five-acre piece of barren earth with three large brick buildings. This is where some of the stone-carvers work, and where blocks of marble are sliced into thin tiles for export to hotels and homes worldwide.

Most of the carvers are in the open field, where hundreds of pieces of marble are being chipped by hand into dozens of interesting shapes. Scattered here and there amid piles of marble flakes are Buddha heads about the size of basketballs. Then, there is a row of marble Peking ducks. And next to them, three men in the traditional Mao Tse-Tung blue worker's clothes are polishing a 10-foot-high vase with koi carved on its side.

The workers in this distant landscape are Mongolian. Their eyes are narrow between puffy lids, their eyebrows high and bushy. Their broad faces and high cheek bones give them the look of American Eskimos. Their hair is thick and black and blown into geometric shapes by the cold, dry wind that is blowing south from Siberia.

The only sound is of the carving, as a hundred metal hammers hit a hundred metal chisels, which connect with the marble simultaneously: *kink king kink king kink kink kink.*

(Opposite page) The small village of Yang Ping in northern China has produced marble pieces for more than 2000 years, mined from pits like this one. The huge blocks of marble are hauled by hand out of the quarry, and then loaded onto a cart which is pulled the two miles to the carving yard by donkey.

(Following pages) Approximately 350 carvers work in two large fields. Although most are 20 to 30 years old, some of the families have been carving marble for 80 generations. Salaries vary according to experience and ability, averaging under $5 dollars a day.

(Opposite page) Most of the workers still favor the blue work clothes of the Communist revolution, like the man in this picture is wearing. Change has been slow to come to these remote parts, but some of the younger generation is beginning to appreciate bright clothing, not allowed in China until recently.

(Above) The master carver and his red pencil. One of the few spots of color in a bleak landscape.

*(Both pages) The huge camphorwood carving of the Chinese
warrior which stands overlooking Kauai Lagoons was also created
in northern China. Blocks of wood are laminated together to create
such a large piece, but it will then be polished and painted so that
it appears as if it were carved from a single piece of wood.*

The Art of Collecting Art:
BALI

(Opposite page) Rice terraces at harvest time in Bali.

(Following pages) The Balinese landscape is dramatic and wonderfully mystical to the Western imagination. The arts which are born of this landscape are diverse and rich. Above, a lone fisherman takes in a lavish dusk, as the sun goes down behind Bali's famed Tanah Lot sea temple.

*Another mystic Balinese landscape reveals Ulu Danu Temple
floating on Lake Bratan, one of Bali's volcanic lakes.*

*Bali's people aren't much impressed by cars. They live relatively
simple lives, bicycling or walking most everywhere they go.*

147

Bali: A Country of Artists

The best-known and uniquely Balinese art forms are in the fields of puppetry and dance. Before foreign artists started visiting the island in the first half of this century, the two-dimensional, or flat, art mainly was derived from puppetry. No surprise, they often showed people dancing.

Usually these figures were drawn on crudely made cloth, using natural materials such as plants and oil lamp soot for paint. The pictures were simple, resembling cartoon strips.

In the 17th century, a rajah commissioned one of the artists to create a work for his palace. That caused the first boom in Balinese art, as others in the ruling aristocracy, as well as commoners, began displaying art in their homes.

However, it wasn't until 1927 that outside influences appeared which led the local artists toward the kind of Balinese painting we see today.

The first important painter to arrive was the German adventurer Walter Spies, one of several Westerners to "discover" Bali. During the 1920s and 1930s, Spies did for Bali what Gauguin did for Tahiti—he presented to the Western world a newfound center of Pacific sensuality and exotica.

Spies lived in Bali for 13 years and during that time, the local artists began picking up his technique and mimicking his fanciful, surrealistic style.

The Dutch artist Rudolf Bonnet arrived during the same period and contributed an exacting, draftsman-like influence. The result was a school of painting that flourishes today, producing large, meticulously plotted canvasses packed full of plants, animals, birds and human figures engaged in a variety of activities.

The crowded pictures—still frequently painted on cloth—at first were called "folk art" by critics in the West. In recent years, the distinct style and composition has attracted a large audience and the paintings are now being created for both museums and a growing international trade.

Art is regarded quite oddly in Bali, by Western standards. Leonard Lueras in his book *Bali: The Ultimate Island* writes, "Formally expressed, art in Bali, whether of *wayang* or Western derivation and influence, is simply a graphic manifestation of ritual behavior that has long been encouraged by the Balinese community, their complex religion and the personal spiritual drive that such factors release in individuals and the collective community.

"Art on this island is not—as is so often the case in most urban communities—a special, creative domain occupied by a select cadre of individuals called artists (and art critics). Nor is it an acceptable symptom of mutant behavior, the manifestation of a misunderstood neurosis, or some mythical free-fire zone visited only by spiritually-inspired visionaries.

"Indeed, anthropologists like to point out that the Balinese language does not even have a word to identify what Western dictionaries define as 'art.'"

(Opposite page) This craftsman is carving temple guardians from stone.

(Following pages) The paintings of Bali are remarkable for their exacting, draftsmanlike quality. Frequently, they mix exotic birds, ripe fruit and thick foliage. In this piece, Java sparrows, butterflies, and crested cockatoos play in a banana tree.

The Art of Collecting Art:
THAILAND

(Opposite page) Wat Suan Doc, Chiang Mai.

(Following pages) The chedi of one of Sukhothai's ancient temples reflected in a lilypond.

Craftsmen have been shaping the exquisite art of Thailand for centuries. The Thai artists are particularly proficient with stylized bronze and wood creations.

Hanging in the Palace Court Galleria at The Westin
Kauai—thousands of miles from its place of origin—is the
elaborately carved teak relief being shaped in this photograph.
Many carvings of this nature are produced in the northern Thai
city of Chiang Mai, near the Burmese border.

A Visit to the Bronze Foundry

In an open lot near the "factory's" main structure, the artists prepared to pour the molten bronze. It was dusk, getting dark. They lifted the heavy ladles and carefully filled the waiting molds, creating an extra-terrestrial glow in the fading Bangkok light.

The smell was pungent, like electrical wires sparking, mixed with the odor of melting wax. And the heat was blistering, causing the skin to bubble with sweat.

Bronze made of copper and tin is the oldest alloy known to man. People learned to make it about 4000 B.C. The period in history between the Stone Age and the Iron Age is known as the Bronze Age because bronze was commonly used to cast containers such as cups, urns and vases. They also shaped bronze into battle axes, helmets, knives, shields and swords.

It is not cheap to make. Consequently, artisans in Thailand today are always looking for cost-saving shortcuts and imaginative sources. Cheaper lead is often added to the mix and at many workshops and factories, much of the metal is obtained by melting old motorcycle radiators.

Bronze is a favorite of sculptors because of its hardness and durability. Statues and bells made of bronze weather to a beautiful brown or develop a green patina characteristic of copper. After such films form, bronze corrodes very slowly, so bronze articles frequently last hundreds of years.

Many such objects are exhibited in The Westin Kauai. There are large, ornately decorated "rain drums" from Chiang Mai, so called because they are left in the garden to catch the thunder of the falling rain. There are European-styled statues baked to a golden brown. And there are greener bronze Buddha and guardian figures in the style found in Thailand's many temples.

All were made using the complex "lost-wax" process, which dates back to antiquity. (Much modern jewelery is also made this way.) First, the original figure is made, using any medium the artist chooses, then a "negative" mold is made from the figure, just as is done reproducing most sculptures.

At this stage, the process deviates, however. The inside of the mold is coated with a thin layer of wax, and the mold is filled with a mixture of plaster and sawdust. The whole thing is packed in clay and baked in high heat. This melts the wax, creating a space between the clay exterior and the plaster core.

This space is then filled with molten bronze and left to cool, after which the clay is carefully chipped away and the soft interior core is removed through a hole left in original mold. That hole is then patched and the finished piece is polished.

Thus has been created a thing of great beauty and strength—an object whose thin skin lends the extreme hardness of the metal a delicate sense of fragility.

(Opposite page) The glow of the molten metal being poured into clay molds creates an other-worldly glow. Later, the clay is chipped away revealing the form of the art piece.

The bronze factory on the outskirts of Bangkok.
The workers are paid by the number of pieces they produce,
and they share in their employer's profits. Thus, the hours they
work stretch into the night.

ABOUT THE COLLECTION

The Masks of Papua New Guinea

The people of the Sepik River region of Papua New Guinea are renown for the great variety of visually powerful art forms which they contribute to the arts of Oceania. The masks and other ceremonial carvings seen along the Harbor Tower Walkway at The Westin Kauai are representative of that tradition, a tradition that has been sought after and appreciated by major museums and private collectors since the late 19th century.

Generally, the masks and carvings represent mythological heroes who were active in the creation of the world, and who played an important role teaching the people of the Sepik River area the knowledge of their culture. These masks and other art forms are still respected today as reminders of the origins of mankind and the wisdom of the social order.

There are also other, often more fantastic, images which represent various spirit entities which dwell in the forests, swamps and rivers. These potentially powerful forces can be either supportive or destructive. Some figurative sculptures represent the real ancestors of the people and recognize their presence and influence in daily life.

Depending on how they were made, masks could represent ancestors, bush spirits, or culture heroes. They would appear at ceremonies initiating young men into adulthood, ceremonies to assure the continued fertility of the land and its people, special ceremonies to deal with sickness, or ceremonies to celebrate the building of a new house or a large canoe.

Many of the objects in The Westin Kauai collection were made by the Iatmul people of the middle region of the Sepik River, roughly 150 miles from the river-mouth along Papua New Guinea's north coast. The Iatmul use three major styles in representing the human face and human-like spirits. The first style is the 'naturalistic' skull type, consisting of painted skulls of dead ancestors and enemies. The second style is a flat, broad face used in most wood carvings and *awan* masks, representing the clan as a provider. The third style is the *mwai* type masks.

The collection showcases many mwai masks. These long, elliptical masks are symbolically decorated with various patterns, painted in earth tones with natural dyes. The upswept eyes and long nose extensions, ending in a totemic animal, are characteristic of mwai masks.

Of the three major styles used in Iatmul culture, the mwai masks seem to represent the more aggressive and masculine aspects of the clan. In ceremony, these masks are attached to conical frames placed over the dancers' heads, while their bodies are concealed under long fiber skirts.

Besides the Iatmul, there are more than 20 other tribal groups in the Sepik region, each with their own distinctive culture and approach to art and artistic expression. This great variety of art and ideas combine to make the Sepik region one of the most aesthetically fertile areas on earth.

(Opposite page) The Sepik River area of Papua New Guinea was one of the last regions on Earth to be visited by modern man. It is, today, one of the world's leading sources of primitive art.

Although many copies are available to the growing Papua New Guinea tourist trade, the authentic dance masks from that region, such as those displayed at The Westin Kauai, are becoming increasingly rare.

Many of the masks were worn in ceremonial dances to portray
clan or tribal spirits. They were attached to conical frames and
placed over the dancers' heads. Their bodies were
concealed under long, fiber skirts.

167

Buddha

Prince Siddartha, known as Shakayamuni Gautama Buddha, was born in 624 B.C. at the foot of the Himalayas, on the border of Nepal. His parents were the children of kings.

At the age of 16 the prince was married to a Brahmin woman and a son was born the following year. By the time the prince was 26, he had several wives and all of the material wealth he wished.

He was not satisfied and, deciding to explore another lifestyle, he left his family and fasted for several years to see if separation from materialism would bring him relief from his misery. It did not. He came to realize that devotion to that extreme was as insulting to the soul as the extremes of his former, material life.

Enlightenment finally came to Siddartha while he was sitting under the Boddhi tree, the tree of knowledge. Thereafter he was Buddha, the Enlightened.

One of the fundamentals emerging from the long meditation that led to enlightenment was that part of life was misery. Another fundamental was that every type of existence came from desire or passion . . . and that only by elimination of that desire could freedom come.

How to accomplish that? By following the Middle Way . . . the Eightfold Path comprised of right opinions, right intentions, right speech, right conduct, right livelihood, right effort, right mindfulness, and right concentration.

Buddhism has been compared to Roman Catholic Christianity for having its own purgatory, a goddess of mercy (Kuan Yin) and its ritual for delivering the dead from pain.

Other similarities include celibacy and fasting, candles and flowers on the altar, incense and holy water, the worship of relics, the canonization of saints, and the use of a dead language in the liturgy.

The trinity of Buddha, past, present and future, is compared to the concept of the Father, Son and the Holy Ghost. The immaculate mother of Buddha was named Maya, similar to that of Mary, mother of Jesus. The 18 Lohan, or Arhats, the followers of Buddha, are compared to the 12 disciples of Christ. The worship of ancestors is compared to saying masses for the dead. The Dalai Lama is compared to the Pope.

Such may only be the ruminations of scholars. Today, Buddhism is one of the world's great religions, with 350 million followers. Most of these are still in Asia, although various Buddhist sects have been embraced in many Western countries.

Buddhism, like Christianity, has stimulated much fine art. Huge Buddhas of limestone, sandstone, marble and every other medium and substance imaginable appear throughout Japan, India, and much of Southeast Asia.

The sculptor generally creates Buddha in one of a number of distinct poses, or mudras. Many are shown in the *samadhi* position, cross-legged with the hands held up, one on top of the other. This is a contemplative, or meditative pose.

If the left hand is held palm down and resting on the knee, Buddha is "calling the earth to witness."

When one or both hands (but usually just the right hand) are held up, thumb and first finger touching, the other three fingers erect, Buddha is teaching.

(Opposite page) This large, marble "healing" Buddha, holding a small medicine jar in his left hand, greets visitors as they first arrive in the porte cochere at The Westin Kauai. Shaped in Yang Ping, it is in the classic style of the T'ang Dynasty (618-906 A.D.).

Buddhist devotee images, such as the one depicted above,
are also a favorite subject of Eastern art. This is one of a pair
from Burma, demonstrating a classic technique wherein the lacquer
surface of the piece is inlaid with hundreds of bits
of mirror and colored glass.

This unusual Buddha image from Thailand is shaped with its halo bordered by elaborate, wing-like appendages, symbolizing flames. The hands are in the classic teaching position of "calling the earth to witness" Buddha's truth.

Another Thai Buddha image, this one in bronze, is also in the
teaching position. Although there are obvious similarities between
Buddha representations, each region and sect depicts Buddha
differently. For instance, the head dress on the Buddha image
above also symbolizes flames, but differs significantly from the
image on the previous page.

(Opposite page) The most common Buddha image in the West is
the "laughing Buddha." Technically, he is not Buddha, but Hotei,
a traveling monk who spread joy and Buddhist doctrine. Often,
people rub his belly for luck.

Bodyguards for the Royal Soul

The royal tombs at Anyang, dating back to China's Shang dynasty (1722-1050 B.C.), contained the bodies of more than 300 sacrificial victims, many of them guards buried with their weapons, or charioteers lying near their chariots and horses.

In time, human sacrifices were replaced with *mingi,* or artistic substitutes. One emperor, Quin Shih Huang Di, who ruled 200 years before Christ, was buried with 8000 life-sized ceramic replicas of his imperial soldiers.

Just as the rulers of China would have guards in life and guardian figures after death, so, too, would temples and government buildings and, eventually, private homes. Many of these figures took animal forms. Today, throughout the Buddhist world, as well as in the West, a pair of guardian lions is commonplace beside a gate or door.

The lion is sacred to Buddhism, and in a style that makes the figures appear dog-like, they are found outside many temples. They always appear at least in pairs, sometimes as mirror images, other times as a male and female. The female is the one playing with a lion cub, while the male has one front paw resting on an embroidered ball.

The lions—or Fo Dogs as they are sometimes called—are to scare away evil demons. For this reason, the creatures are generally quite muscular, with prominent claws and teeth. Bronze lions from Thailand often are inset with bits of mirror, the idea being that when the demons see their reflections, they will be frightened and leave.

Many guardian figures left over from earlier times took mythical human form. In India, for instance, the four Heavenly Guardians—or Deva Kings—guard the temples with a variety of weapons. One brandishes a magic sword capable of producing thousands of lethal spears. Another carries a stringed instrument whose music causes his enemies to burst into flames.

(Opposite page) Guardian images traditionally appear in pairs.
Often they are lions, evoking strength and courage. They are seen
on either side of a doorway, guarding whatever is inside.

*The conventional Chinese lion is sometimes called the
Dog of Fo. Another common Western version of the name
is Foo Dog. The left paw of the female traditionally rests on her
cub's head, as shown above.*

Guardian figures also took human form, as does this Chinese
wood carving, which stands as part of a quartet of such figures at
The Westin Kauai. Each of the four hold a symbolic object. This
figure holds a lute, the most honorable of all instruments, capable
of restraining all evil passions.

The Sensual Story of Kuan Yin

Kuan Yin is one of the most profound and revered figures in Buddhism, whose story is generally misunderstood.

Her origins in India are as a male figure called Avalokitisvara, born from a beam of light emanating from Buddha's eye. In India, as Buddhism was finding its early popularity, Avalokitisvara became known for his compassion.

Through many incarnations he lived, earning a place in nirvannah. Nonetheless, he turned away to return to the earth as a Bodhisattva to teach Buddhist law—that there is a release from suffering—and the nature of that release.

The change in sexual identity and the name change to Kuan Yin occurred in China in the 7th century. It also came about deliberately, when a priest translated the Indian name to mean "Hearer of the Sounds (of the cries of the world)." It was also said that, first in Tibet and then in China, a female deity of compassion was felt to be a necessity.

Whatever the reason, or cause, Avalokitisvara was now Kuan Yin, a male had become female, and the new, revitalized and redefined deity was at the center of a cult that included many non-Buddhists.

Consequently, she was given great power and respect. She was compared, in later years, to the Virgin Mary. Young married couples prayed to her for children, pregnant women for sons, mothers for the health of those born.

Some say this identification with children coincided with the arrival in the Orient of the Portuguese, who brought Christian figures of the madonna and child. From this time forward, many figures of Kuan Yin included small children.

In China, her story sometimes is reduced to a simple folk tale, in which she defied her father's wish that she marry. Consequently, she was sent to a monastery where she was forced to cook and wash for 500 nuns. When her father heard that the birds and beasts did her chores for her, he burned the monastery and ordered her strangled.

There followed a period of time in the "world below." After that, came the Peace of Immortality and enthronement as Bodhisattva. Finally, when she heard of her father's terminal illness, curable only by a potion made from the eyes and hands of a living person, she plucked out one of her eyes and had her hands cut off. Her father was healed and thus became a Buddhist.

True believers are angered by such tales. Rightly, they cling to a more serious interpretation and point to the many symbols identified with the goddess. The lotus, known for its many seeds and consequent fruitfulness, frequently is included in the sculpture. So, too, the image of the pearl, which is regarded as the "concrete essence of the moon distilled through the secret workings of the Female Principle, Yin."

(Opposite page) The goddess of mercy, Kuan Yin, is always depicted in a similar fashion. As shown here, she wears an elaborate hair style, and a headpiece with a lotus blossom in the center.

Often, Kuan Yin is depicted sitting atop a lion, as she is in this exquisite blue and white porcelain. Her posture represents her supremacy over the forces of nature. This figure is in the style of the Ming Dynasty (1368-1644 A.D.)

(Opposite page) The Kuan Yin figure beneath the banyan tree in The Westin Kauai's Palace Court is a marble from China. Kuan Yin is a Bodhisattva, assured of enlightenment, but remaining on Earth as a teacher. This figure was carved in the sensual style of the T'ang Dynasty (618-906 A.D.)

The beautiful Nawiliwili Bay features gentle surf, warm water, blue skies, and one of the world's grand resorts: The Westin Kauai.

ACKNOWLEDGEMENTS

Robyn Buntin (Robyn Buntin of Honolulu) and Mary Snodgrass, for help in identifying and describing the Asian art.

Kepa Maly (The Westin Kauai Resort) for providing so much information about the history and legend of old Hawaii.

W. Dudley Child, Jr. of InterIsland Resorts, for sharing memories and photographs.

Bernice Pauahi Bishop Museum and the Kaua'i Museum for assistance in historical research.

Hand-coloring of photographs on Pages 50, 56 & 57 by Robert Sablan.

PHOTO CREDITS

Pages 52, 56 & 57, Bernice Pauahi Bishop Museum; Pages 50, 58, 60, 63, 64 & 65, Kauai Museum; Page 68, W. Dudley Child, Jr.

Grand Resorts of the World logo by Linda Fong.